Before Forty After 9/11

Poems From the Heart (Land)

By

Tony Bethel

ISBN: 1-4033-8714-1 (e-book)
ISBN: 1-4033-8715-X (Paperback)

This book is printed on acid free paper.

1stBooks – rev. 01/21/03

Put Him Number One:

Put Him number one, in everything you do.

Put Him number one, and it will come to you.

Put Him number one, when in worry, when in doubt.

Put Him number one, and be assured — He will help you out.

Put Him number one, before you and me.

Put Him number one, and your soul shall forever run free.

Tony Bethel

Poet

I am the poet, the one who writes and thinks as well.

The one who contemplates heaven and hell.

The one who seeks the depth of the soul.

The one who lifts men's spirits from their holes.

I am the poet, listen and see, for my words shall set you free.

I am the one who will nourish your heart, challenge your brain, and give your spirit a start.

I am the one you seek in your hour of need; when middle class values center on greed.

I am the one you want to hear when the body is weary of drugs, sex, and beer.

I am the one who you turn to in doubt.

When you ask, "Is there a God?" — My words seek him out.

Yes, I am the poet for better or worse. I set the mind, body, and spirit free, through wit, rhyme, and verse.

When The Poets Cease To Write

When the poets cease to write there will be darkness instead of light. No moon to light up the night. No sun shining bright – when the poets cease to write.

When the poets cease to write the nations shall continue to fight, but no inspiration or insight shall they have. The wise men shall laugh, for they will realize man's mistakes – when he kills his brother, his soul shall be as fire on the lake. The thunder will roar and the Earth will shake — when the poets cease to write.

When the poets cease to write man will have lost his sight and forever blind shall he be, when words cease to arouse thee. Words are like tiny morsels blest – when devoured they enlighten the breast and up lift the soul, opening the self and filling the holes.

The holes of loneliness. The holes of despair. The holes of abandonment. The holes of "I don't care". The holes of anger. The holes of violence. The holes of death. The holes of silence.

When the poets cease to write, the world will be very dull, the stars shall fall from out the sky and mere mortals shall wonder why? But the poets, the poets, they know, they know.

Spring Again

It is the time of the lion. The time of the lamb, the time of Aries the ram. Yes, March is here and spring has come, the buds are green, ripening under the sun. The morning dew is fresh and wet. Where winter once conquered now shows signs of retreat. The snow now melts and winter releases its clasp, It must now wait for another chance. The March wind whips the trees, they whirl and dance in the breeze.

Lovers are able to walk again, hand in hand in the gentle rain, sweetly whispering endearing names. Birds chirp above their heads enroute to build nests for their summers stead. Where dead leaves once covered the ground, green bristles of grass pop their heads up as if awakening from a winter's nap. Flowers wrestle their way from the ground, and open their petals as if to embrace the sun.

Spring holds hope for everyone; of a new year begun; like a prodigal son. Spring has come again, to share our lives, and be our friend. Time and time again spring walks out of our lives only to return again.

Tony Bethel

Spring helps us to realize the cycle of life; of joy and pain; of sorrow and hope; of the human heart that tries to cope. Spring again! Spring again! Come into my embrace again! Like a fickle lover you promise to stay, only to go away – leaving me to hope, that you will come back someday.

Connecticut In the Fall:

Connecticut in the fall—the prettiest season of them all.   The leaves have turned from green to brown, bringing a new look to the New England towns.   The sea whips at the bay, the waves crash higher each day, gently tossing a cold silver spray that refreshes me on this cold New England day. The sun shines bright high above the trees, but its "real" warmth never reaches me, for I am entangled amidst a web of trees standing proud and tall. The crisp brown leaves look much more mature by the passing hour, as if old men standing looking at the sun, remembering once that they too were young. My heart is still warm, despite the cutting breeze. The wind whips and whirls through the trees, he whistles his song for me. I feel the bark of the trees and I feel the story of the forest unfold as if a blind man reading braille – my mind has found a lost and wonderous trail. The hawk soars high in the sky, how I envy his view. To fly high above the land – it must look like some great plan; and it is—from the great creator. I see the fawn and the doe that try to hide amongst the trees, their beauty and grace cannot be hid, for their gentleness is of great contrast to the jagged bark and crinkled leaves. I wait until night and sit on a rock over the bay; the view is so tremendous my words cannot convey. The beauty which unfolds before my eyes is such a wonderous surprize. Even though darkness engulfs me, the lights sprinkled and peppered in the distance reminds me of thousands of fireflies busily rushing about, and the bay is like a mirror reflecting those fireflies. My eyes shift to the different ships and boats in the harbor; they are rocking up and down rhythmically as if they were schools of fish surrounding the shore. This and so much more you will have in store, if you see one of the greatest sites of all

—Connecticut in the fall.

Winter's Soul:

It is that time of season when flowers cease to grow.

It is that time of season when the ground is covered with snow.

It is that time of season for birds to travel south again.

It is that time of season to lose a treasured friend.

It is that time of season when the warmth gives up its life.

It is that time of season when the wind cuts like a knife.

It is that time of season to wish again for spring.

It is that time of season to give praise for many things.

It is that time of season that we try to live as one;

As we await the birth of His one and only son.

We think of this time of year for gifts and fancy—never realizing all of our missed chances.

Chances to bring love, chances to bring spring,

Chances to end the winter this season brings, we miss so many chances, and lose so many hopes, it is such a wonder how we humans seem to cope.

Tony Bethel

Even though it is time for winter and the cold engulfs the whole—

let us try to prevent the penetration of the soul.

Words:

Words can be so profound.

Words can make one so proud.

Words can raise the spirit's soul

Words can drive one into holes.

Words can open doors ajar.

Words can close one's mind so far.

Words are bits and pieces new.

Words travel from me to you.

WORDSMITH

He is called the wordsmith, his tools – the pencil and pen; he forges the thoughts, emotions, and actions of all feeling men.

He is called the wordsmith, his room is his workshop where words of steel are set aglow in the fiery furnace which flows. The flow of ideas. The flow of punctuation. The flow of concepts. The flow of enunciation.

The mind is a furnace where ideas are smelted, touching others' hearts 'till they are melted. Hear him forging words in the distance, hammering with delight, creating the phrase that fits just right.

Wordsmith! Wordsmith! Hammer your words well. Inspire us! Save us from Hell! Hammer your mighty pen upon your iron pad, let the sparks of ideas flow from your head. Lift us, take us to your level of delight. Your work shall live forever. Your craft give us sight.

Mom's Loving Black Hands

Thinking of those loving black hands which raised me from a boy to a man.

Thinking of those loving black hands which spanked me often when I went against her plans.

Thinking of those loving black hands which prepared greens, black-eyed peas, chit'lins, biscuits and gravy, chicken and fish – my mom cooked soul food as well as gourmet dishes.

Thinking of those loving black hands I held so much, I remember the energy drawn, from their very touch.

Thinking of those loving black hands which tilled the earth of our small patch of land. On that loving black hand was a magic green thumb, that raised many things, including two sons.

I think often of those loving black hands, because of them, I am a better man.

BE STRONG MY BLACK BROTHERS:

Be strong my Black Brothers! Who are as dark as night don't give up the struggle, don't relinquish the fight.

Be strong my Black Brothers! You must'nt have fear because the day of triumph is slowly drawing near.

Be strong my Black Brothers! Strive long and hard we must have discipline to gain our rewards.

Be strong my Black Brothers! And respect your women remember, your mother was once your age too.

Be strong my Black Brothers! And Unify NOW let us stop bickering and produce gains – Now!

Be strong my Black Brothers! There's no need to dread Even though lynched, burned and tortured we still are not dead.

Be strong my Black Brothers! And lift your head high. Do not lower yourselves to a moan and a sigh.

Be strong my Black Brothers! Listen to my heed-"let STRENGTH and DISCIPLINE be your strongest creeds!

Be strong my Black Brothers! And be NOT ashamed that our forefathers came here clothed only in chains.

Look upon our misfortunes as some unrelenting quest in which we STILL prove that we CAN outlast the rest.

Tony Bethel

YOU HAVE MANY BLACKS

I was once asked to say what it's like to be Black to tell the truth,

its not as simple as that.

You have many Blacks whose color differs from mine.

You have many Blacks with a different concept of time.

You have many Blacks who are frustrated in many ways.

You have many Blacks who will not eat today.

You have many Blacks forced to face the cold.

You have many Blacks without adequate homes.

You have many Blacks whose hearts are broken.

You have many Blacks who are simply tokens.

You have many Blacks who seek the truth.

You have many Blacks with the loyalty of Ruth.

You have many Blacks in confusion and despair.

You have many Blacks who are in control and aware.

You have many Blacks who are paranoid of their color.

You have many Blacks who call each other BROTHER.

You have many Blacks and each one is different from me.

So open your mind and the truth shall set you free.

Fathers and Sons:

Every generation a man promises to be good to his son, yet, the dream dies one by one.

What makes it so difficult for fathers and sons; as each day is ended, a new one is begun.

In the same light, why can't each forgive his own, then there could be peace within the home.

Fathers expect so much from their sons, yet, sons want to be what their father was once.

Fathers fail to understand that they were young too. The circle is unbroken returning to you.

Age upon age, and cycle upon cycle, fathers love their sons or else they would not take care of them. But yet in his eternal love a father ends up scaring his son. A son only wants what is his and his alone. To grow into a man — a noble father, like his own.

Tony Bethel

A Letter From A Friend

A letter from a distant friend. My eyes once dry are wet again.
For in my mind is the memory, of her sweet love that embraces me.
Embraces me and keeps me warm, brightens the night and calms the
storm. A letter not sweet of fragrant perfume, but sweet of her love
that drips like dew. Was it a letter of love? Was it a letter of
friendship? Was it a letter of concern? Just to be in her presence
makes my heart burn. Burn with the ecstacy of desire. Burn with the
most furious of fires. Longing to fondle her curly locks and kiss the
slender neck which tilts back in a graceful tease which brings my
heart to its knees. How could one letter do this to me, bind my heart
and encage me. I think of those times we sat a heartbeat away, yet
worlds apart, eons away. Yet at times the sea parts our love, I still
feel your warmth as in the breast of the dove. I long to hold you in
my arms, yet shy away for fear, that one embrace would cause you to
disappear. For if I hold you too tight will not love slip away? Yet if I
hold you in my mind our love is rekindled each and every day. Take
my kiss in your mind for my love will always be there. Take my

heart in your mind for it is already there. Take my soul in your mind

and I will be there.

Friendship

I make a toast to friendship. I make a toast to you. I make a toast to things most dear, which tend to be so few.

I talk about our friendship, a rare sight to behold, for it transcends sex, race, creed, color, and gold. For I am not as rich as you, nor have I ever been, but with a friendship such as ours, my wealth outshines a king. It was you who showed me how to live, laugh and how to be. It was you who truly set my captive spirit free.

Free from the chains of loneliness; free from the tortures of stress free from the hole of despair; free once again, to love again.

Friendship is such a lovely thing, it lifts the soul on eagles wings; it withstands the tests of time; is more sweeter than the sweetest wines.

It is our friendship of which I speak which I hope will never peak.

For I know it will only get higher, and deliver me from the fire.

The fire of hate, anguish, and greed.

The fire of jealousy, envy, and need.

Friendship knows no bounds, it is beautiful music – such colorful sounds. Special shall friendship always be, as long as it is shared between you and me

Tony Bethel

A Friend's Pain

A time of sorrow. A time of pain. A very dear friend is hurt again.

How to relieve? How to sooth?

I do not know which way to move.

Loyalty binds us closer together.

Never forget that we are brothers.

He Is Often In My Thoughts

He is often in my thoughts when I think of times ahead. When the sky is blue. When I think of you.

He is often in my thoughts when I think about this world about the death and destruction which has now unfurled.

He is often in my thoughts when I am wondering if I am saved. Is he really our master? Are we really his slaves?

He is often in my thoughts when I commit a sin, I feel as one who has lost points, and must begin again.

He is often in my thoughts when I think of a heaven; with all the wickedness in the world is anyone worth saving?

He is often in my thoughts when I think of a hell; for with all the warnings he gives, man wishes for his soul to sell.

He is often in my thoughts when I think of death, and all the unfinished business of life I have left.

He is often in my thoughts when I think of the resurrection. For only through his love can we hope for redemption.

Tony Bethel

On Your Wings:

Lift me high upon your wings, where I will laugh, pray, and sing.

I listen to your gentle voice, that has given me the greatest choice.

The choice of freedom. The choice of love.

The choice of your spirit from above.

Lift me high upon your wings, and save me from these evil things:

The evils of lust. The evils of strife. The evils of the pain we must

face in this life.

Lift me high above the rest, so they will know, you are the best.

In your love you will find mine

   —and it will last throughout all time.

He Walks With Me.

He walks with me when skies are grey.

He walks with me when I lose my way.

He walks with me throughout the night.

He helps me through my hardest fights.

He walks with me slow or fast.

He knows my pace, from the past.

He walks with me and when I fall, his guiding hand lifts me tall.

He walks with me everyday.

He knows my life and knows my ways.

He walks with me, though him I cannot see.

My wish is to walk with him; rather than for him to walk with me.

Tony Bethel

What's In A Name

We call him many names, but the meaning stays the same. We look for a resurrection, for a cross – a holy section. We try hard with all our might to follow the path we think is right. Buddhist, Hindu, Moslem, Jew, the world will end regardless of you.

Tolerate your fellow man, reach out your helpful hand. Shy not away from me because I practice a different creed.

Live, read, and understand that I am just a normal man whose religion differs from yours, but whose heart bleeds – like yours.

Don't shut out the love within – for is that not a mortal sin. Instead I say practice your preachings, love your brothers and follow your teachings.

Comprehend the world at hand, for it is filled with many a man. Islamic, Christian and Jew, Catholic, Buddhist, and Hindu. Many religions on our planet.

So many beliefs I cannot understand it. We are so different, yet so much the same I think the main difference lies in the name.

Let us end the destruction. Let us start a new life – free from pain, destruction and strife. Let us live as brothers, as God has planned, to work together and fulfill his plan.

No matter how you look at it, we believe the same, but we are separated…by a name.

Tony Bethel

Man Made?

To be a man, to be a man, was it ever in God's plan for a man to prove himself to the world, burden himself and grow cold. To lock out others emotionally to never know what love means.

To be a man, to be a man, was it ever in God's plan for men to go off to wars. To kill and die robbing stores, to live in slums and poverty, to be a victim of society, to be an outcast or pariah, looking for a new messiah- in sex, drugs and booze; dear brothers you could only lose.

To be a man, To be a man, was it ever in God's plan for man to dominate, discriminate, subjugate, hate and eliminate his fellow man.

To be a man, to be a man, was it ever in God's plan – to store bombs instead of food. To kill blacks, browns, whites, reds, yellows, arabs and jews. To know the humiliating stench of rotting human flesh, rather than the innocent sweet smell of the rose.

To be a man, to be a man, was it ever in God's plan for men to build their bodies beyond belief, to curse and scoff the "lesser ones", not realizing we are all God's sons.

To be a man, to be a man, was it ever in God's plan, for man to suffer total destruction, after Christ's resurrection. To have the world crumble apart, to grow perverted, with a hardened heart, to distort love and sex, and make them one. To regard women as "toys" and "fun". To tell a child white lies and blind their innocent eyes.

To parade around a moral code, that when under pressure could never hold. To party all night long, stagger in at the break of dawn – then, wonder what is wrong?

Lord is anything as You planned. So many chances You have given man in this world You made. So far from perfection, yet God-made, or should I say "Man-Made."

For Eternity?

In times of trouble we call his name. When we feel stress doubt or pain. In times of trouble we call his name, when we are in grief, mourn or strain. We look to him with heavy hearts – hoping he will relieve us, and help our hearts.

In times of trouble we call his name, when we are degraded, exploited or ashamed. We yell to him to free us, help us, hear us, see us. We ask for things all the time, hoping he will deliver – on time. We make demands upon our God, yet when we sin we are stained with blood. We yell at each other in desperation, get frustrated with exasperation, yet pray to our God with total elation. How can we love who we have never seen; when we hate our neighbor, hurling insults that are mean. How can we enter God's house on Sunday, only to sin the following Monday. If we love God as we say, we would love him everyday, not just when it is convenient for "me", or if he is giving us something for free. Why do we yell at our brothers, sisters, aunts, uncles, fathers and mothers, when we should realize how much we need one another. For if that mother leaves today, where will you go,

and who will you pay, for that mother of yours has gone to God –
ever more to stay. Remember dear friends we are all family, and
should strive for unity, and when God sees this, he will be with us for
eternity.

When I am all Alone

When I am all alone I think of your face and of your tender young body which I want to embrace.

When I am all alone I think only of you and your sweet gift of love that always pulls me through.

When I am all alone it is you that I miss; Your sweet conversation, your passionate kiss.

When I am all alone it is you that I adore; for if I could live forever, I could never love you more.

When I am all alone my mind is very still, yet, the thoughts of you come often — against my will.

When I am all alone I want to scream and shout. I want to release this passion which must have a way out.

When I am all alone there is no place to go, for no matter where… You are always there.

When I am all alone my feelings I postpone, to when you will be, all alone with me.

Sing a Song:

Sing a song of joy, sing a song of laughter.

Sing a song of rebirth; of this world and hereafter.

Sing a song of life. Sing a song of hope.

Sing a song of triumph, and the spirit which forever copes.

Sing a song of faith and merriment abound. Leave your sorrows in

the bitter cold, let love flourish like a loud thunderous sound.

Sing a song of family which makes the spirit strong.

Sing a song of Christmas – the whole day long.

Sing a song of wonder, sing a song of cheer, sing a song of patience,

for our Savior now is here.

Sing a song of Easter and do not mourn or cry, for our Saviour who is

gone will come again – never more to die.

Sing a song for each and every day, as we all hope, care, pray, and

wait for that miraculous day.

Try a Little Gentleness:

Try a little gentleness when things don't go your way.

Try a little gentleness when the Sun does not shine today.

Try a little gentleness when your boss shouts in your ear.

Try a little gentleness when your child sheds a tear.

Try a little gentleness when the lady tells you no.

Try a little gentleness when you hold her close.

Try a little gentleness when you ask for things you want.

Try a little gentleness when you use the things you have got.

Try a little gentleness each and every day...

Because gentle Jesus died, for *our* ungentle ways.

Death Waits For Me

Death waits for me at the end of the hall; from the grave I hear his morbid call.

Death waits for me in the depths of the sea, resounding waves call for me.

Death waits for me in the heat of the fire; in the impulses of man; at the seat of desire.

Death waits for me and is a patient friend, who walks with thee until life's road has ended.

Death waits for me upon the mount; I try to avoid him, but he seeks me out.

Death waits for me each and every day, his embrace gets tighter as I try to pull away.

Death waits for me as my body is laid into the grave – I have ceased to be Life's unhappy slave.

Death waits for me for an eternity, and only his touch can set me free(?)

Another Bad Dream!?

Up and down across the sea sailing in a submarine. Wondering what is next out there? Wondering how to defend ourselves?

In and out, dodge and swerve, diving deep, and making curves. Sailing through the ocean blue, for democracy, for me and you.

Surface! Surface! Come up top. Periscope swings and stops. Focus on the enemy – is it them? Or is it me?! Fire one! No regrets. The world is safe – once again.

Oh but now, a full-scale war. Mass destruction, more and more. Bloodied babies die in arms; screaming mothers all around. Men once strong, are blown away – never more for happy days.

Wake up! Wake up! Just another bad dream. Let us strive for peace- So this won't be.

Just A Horny Squid

Here I am facing the breeze, sailing across the seven seas. To be in your embrace again—to know again a long lost friend. As the waves pull me closer, I think of your lips as sweet as ambrosia. I taste them in my mind—Imagination can be so unkind. It brings me to you, and you to me, but it does not satisfy the sensations in me. It leaves the heart hungry and cold, like a hungry lion missing a sleek young goat. As the wind whips at the sails, I think of your dark black hair, and skin of golden brown, of your youthful breasts—so firm and round. I think of your body so close to mine, of your soft, round, firm behind; of that sensual glow, that tells me what I need to know. As the sun beams down from on high, I think of your smile that could light up the night, of your personality so bright, I cannot wait for tonight. To hold you deep within my arms; to fill you with a sailor's charms. To tell you of stories from far away; to make love to you, each and everyday. To wake up in the morning's light, and see such a beautiful sight; lying in between the sheets like a warm, tender sandwich,

Tony Bethel

waiting to be eaten. My desires never seem to quit—I guess I am just

a horny squid.

How Should I Feel?

I visited the shopping mall and saw the decorations on the wall. The Evergreens so tall the bright colored Christmas lights almost made me fall. I saw Santa in his red & white suit with his cottony white beard and bright black boots. I saw the glowing Christmas fire. I saw the eight reindeer – a sight to behold, with their soft brown skins and their horns of gold. I then "saw" my son who would not have such fun, because he was in Afghanistan. How should I feel about the Nativity scene, when I see the Virgin Mary's fluorescent gleam – about her one and only son who gave his life so we could live as one. I look in her eyes and wonder if she knew of the pain and anguish he would go through. It seemed so pointless for him to die, when I make the comparison, I want to cry. Will my son return in this life or must I too suffer in pain and strife. When I see the commercials, advertisements, gimmicks and deals they all seem to be so unreal. But then again, how should I feel?

Tony Bethel

Time To Leave Again

I cannot feel the words, they leave my throat dry. I cannot feel the sounds, my eyes want to cry. Away we must go again, no time for delay. Away we must go again on our "merry" way. Thoughts of you won't leave me be. Thoughts of you that my eyes want to see. Alone again. Leaving again. Crying again. Sad again. Depression sets in. Only one good part about leaving – knowing I will see you again the following season.

In 1984

I see the world on the verge of destruction, but man's only concern is mass production (of nuclear arms).

I ask myself what to think when others are killed for being theirselves, We live in a technical society, but can you tell me ... if you're free?

I wonder about these things... am I wrong to non-conform. Is it right to live your life a robot, a cog in THE machine.

Our society is Soooo "clean"!

Sanitized

Mechanized

Industrialized

And all other Lies.

We live in a time of FOOLS; those whose intellect is beyond me, yet behind me. Why can't "man" wait for me to catch up? Yet, why is "man" so far behind "me" ("you").

This society with its emphasis on MONEY, SEX, and MATERIALS…

Is it worth it????

My heart burns, but my tongue is silent!

My ears long to hear, but are deafened by the sound.

I want to listen, but the message is all wrong.

THIS society is not for us.

"man" is a sheep; constantly being led, but NOT taking the lead.

Why repeat the same mistakes twice?

repeat the same mistakes twice?

the same mistakes twice?

same mistakes twice?

mistakes twice?

more than twice?

The Shroud

Sitting here a blank comes over my mind – loneliness can be so unkind. To be lonely in the crowd is like wearing a black shroud. Thinking of you hurts so bad. Makes me anxious, makes me sad, makes me think of the times we had.

I look in the mirror and what do I see – a lonely man of 23, Always wondering why, I am a "lonely guy".

Wishing to be accepted – wishing for love, but the wish never seems to come true, then I am left with the haunting thoughts of you. Why must your memory torture me.

Come back and break these chains which bind me. For it is your love that has opened my heart. Like a lock and key, your love has made me free. Yet unannounced and unproclaimed, you seem to have forgotten my name, and my love wilts on the vine – waiting for time. They say time heals all wounds, but time's relief will not come in time. Here I sit with my back against the light blue sky, which shines rays of hope instead of questioning why?

Loneliness is like a green, slimy, sticky goo, which attaches to your heart and refuses to let go. Thoughts of you crash through my mind, shattering my future, and the past resurfaces… a second time.

When will your spirit leave me? When can I be free? When shall I enjoy loves pleasures once more? Thinking of you depresses me. For when I think of you I think of the sun, of the moon, of sweet dreams to come. When I think of you I get a new high, a new plateau, new wings to fly. When I think of you, I think of the freshness of the morning dew, of the pretty birds singing in spring, of many new and beautiful things. Your smile is like a rainbow which lights up the sky, but without your presence the world is dark – I want to die. Why are you so cold? Why do you refuse my advances? Why can't you think of love and the numerous chances?

Chances to be happy. Chances to be free. Chances to spend your life loving me. For is that such a horrid thought? Without your love, my heart is in drought. Your love refreshes me like the morning sun, like the evening rain, for in your love there is no guilt, no pain – I am reborn again.

Tony Bethel

Come back and free me from the crowd; give me your love and
lift the shroud.

Be Not Bitter About Love

Be not bitter about love – that awesome four-letter word that few have ever seen and oh so many have heard.

Be not bitter about love and its sweet and tempting smell, that has often ripped men's hearts and sentenced them to hell.

Be not bitter about love for like a flower dies in winter – it returns again in spring.

Be not bitter about love – with all its frill and glamour that will often grill you and leave you in a clamor.

Be not bitter about love like a circle never beginning, and which has no end, love puts on the facade of a long lost friend – and ah, alas, my heart is broken again.

Be not bitter about love with all its woe and dread – Because?

you

    could

        be

           six feet

              under

very

cold

and

dead.

I Love You

How can I say what cannot be said.

Your love is beyond all compare.

Your beauty so fair.

Tell me where to go- I will be there.

For your love I will do anything.

For it is your love that means everything.

I love you.

Your Love Is Like

Your love is like a mountain stream; cool, refreshing, a beautiful dream.

Your love is like a pastry treat, warm and tender, fresh and sweet.

Your love is like a bird that soars; an eagle with pride, loyalty, and more.

Your love is like a lion's mane, full of strength and power having no shame.

Your love is like a dream come true, your love has brought my desert a refreshing dew.

Your love is like an endless story, forever beautiful, forever flowing.

Your love is like...

Let It Flow

Don't hold back let it go.

Don't hide it let it show.

Don't keep it in let me know.

Don't destroy it let it grow.

Don't dam it

-let it F

      L

      O

      W

Tony Bethel

At This Time of Year

I look at the glistening snow and it reminds me of your fluorescent glow. I walk the tree-lined path and more memories seem to flash. Memories of life, of love, and of the one God above. I trudge the snow covered hills and I think of the white frills you once wore, and of our romantic Christmas visits to all the merchants' stores. Yes, it's that time of year, the time for cheer. I hear the carollers so clear and I think of the things you used to whisper in my ear; an angel so sweet, a much desired treat. Yes, it's the time of year to put away past fears, a time to think of you my dear. For I have tried and tried but to no avail to perish those thoughts which make me wail. I also remember how you made my heart sail. This is the time of year for love, for gifts, and for the heart and spirit to lift. But you see… without you I am lost. My once brightened smile has lost its gloss. How ironic I feel at this time of year. The things we used to do together. The fun we once had in this weather. Yes, it is the time of year – but my thoughts are not running clear. The decorations which fill our house yet make it bare; because it reminds me of what we had to share, of your skin so fair, of your silky brown hair. Why is life so cruel… death so unfair;

to take a woman I found so dear –

At This Time Of Year.

Beyond

Beyond the trees is the mount.

    Your love reminds me of its summit.

Beyond the mount is the sun.

    Your love reminds me of its warmth.

Beyond the sun is the universe.

    Your love reminds me of its vastness.

Beyond the universe is God.

    I worship your love – as I worship his.

May Your Heart Be Always With Me:

May your heart be always with me when my back is against the wall.

May your heart be always with me when I stumble or I fall.

May your heart be always with me when the wind whips at my face.

May your heart be always with me as I travel place to place.

May your heart be always with me when difficulties rise.

May your heart be always with me when tears of loneliness fill my eyes.

May your heart be always with me during pain and during strife.

May your heart be always with me, at all times within my life.

May your heart be always with me when I lay my head to sleep.

May your heart be always with me, bless me, keep me safe and free.

May your heart be always with me through our arguments and pains, for only with love and patience can love grow again.

Tony Bethel

May your heart be always with me when I fight the battles of the day.

May your heart be always with me when I am tempted to run astray.

May your heart be always with me and help me find a better way.

May your heart be always with me now, forever and always.

It Can Never Be!?

In my heart you shall always be my true love, for within my war-torn soul, you are my peace, you are my dove. Time and time again I have tried to explain my love for you—only to come up short...I have tried in vain. When I think of your beauty, I think of those moonlit nights, those romantic talks, of our hands held tight, thinking about those soft, warm hands, those sensitive eyes—I then turn my head and heave a sigh; realizing my dream was only a lie. Now I am faced with the reality; that a love like ours can never be. We are so far apart; like two distant rivers that wish to intermingle, our distance and destiny will always keep us single. Oh how I have thought of thee, that long brown mane of honey brown, of the tame horse which longs to be wild. Your sweet smell attracts me like a bee, but you are like a closed flower which hides from me. I am like a wanderer in the desert seeking an oasis—Yet a mirage of love appears before my eyes, leaving tears upon my face. For I know the mirage is a lie—Yet the dream shall never die. I long for your embrace, yet wonder why!? For you are just flesh, and so am I. But, I wish to join with you, and

57

will continue to try. There are many things which keep us distant, but distance is the least of these things. Oh, how I wish to love you—the way a man loves a woman; but our desires do not coincide, our fears so great, can we ever try?! We are like two powerful locomotives going in separate, unparalleled directions, two souls longing for affection, but our ambitions and our goals keep us striving for perfection. To reach a plateau of the spirit, of a different type of love, the kind which is shone from above—which encompasses many lights, and shines so bright. I wonder if our lights can mingle, keep us together, yet keep us single. We are two who yearn for love, but our natures prevent us from giving in. One wanting to be lovers, one wanting to be friends. How can I join with thee, for you are the rocks, and I the sea. I am forever pressed against you, but our union can never be!?

Handle with Care

This is for those who have felt love, yet love is not returned. This is for all whose hearts burn while their tongues' are silent. This is for all who eagerly yearn to caress and be caressed, yet are disappointed when love turns its back on them. This is for all who have felt wanton, lustful, passionate desire for someone who does not even notice them. This is for all men who reach for love with their fingertips, and for all women who reach for love with their hearts, and of the difficult paradox that ensues. This is for all of you who wondered "what is wrong with me", because everyone else has someone else and the only else I have is myself. This is for all those unthinking lovers who chose to end their lives, feeling that there is nothing greater in this world than to love – yet find out from the fellow creatures of this world that the most important things in this world is having material wealth, a superficial personality, and an attractive body. It is as if we are the only ones who speak in a world full of mutes and even though our message is so simple – the others cannot hear us or tell us how they want to love and be loved. Why is loving so difficult? Why is it so hard for me to expose myself to you and why is it so hard for you to accept my exposure. It is as if I were naked and wearing a robe and flashed my "true" self in front of you. You, surprised at my honesty, run away frightened at my revelation of self. I runaway, realizing my openness and rejection – waiting within for a chance to reveal my true self to others. Is life to be lived as if those who reveal themselves are the enemies, perverts, and degenerates? Should the emotions always be concealed – the way our genitals are concealed in clothing. If I tell you that I love you, will you make me ashamed? If I expose my vulnerability, will you attack my fortress? If I give myself, will you rob me? These are questions we should ask ourselves. These are things we contemplate. For is not emotions part of our whole being; and if a part does not function will not the whole machine collapse? If I give my hand, will you cut it off? If I give my kiss will you turn away? If I give my embrace will you turn cold? Why is love so difficult – yet so easy? All we have to do is reach out, yet when we reach out we expose ourselves to possible destruction, as if an atom were split, we too would be destroyed. Love is so beautiful yet so dangerous- "Handle with care."

My World

In my world of darkest grey, there is a shade of blue – that is when the thoughts of you come crashing through.

In my world of darkest night, when you are on my mind – there is only light.

In my world of twisted confusion, your love breaks through all illusion.

In my world of massive pressure, your love is a relief valve, that I will always treasure.

In my world of deadly silence, the thought of your warm voice is music to my ears.

In my world of death and destruction, your love is the resurrection.

In my world of deepest secrets, none are hidden from you.

In my world of desperate survival, your love is my life, my revival.

Tony Bethel

In my world, you are my world.

When We Make Love

When we make love it will be with elation, with fulfillment, patience and adoration. It will be in wonder and respect. It will be in beauty and sensation.

When we make love it will last forever, showing my love for you – never ending.

When we make love I will give you all of me, my deepest parts, you have never seen.

When we make love there will not be two but one.

When we make love, may our bodies be blest, and may our love we never test. For when we test love we test hearts and when we test hearts we test a part – not a whole. When we make love may you tell me all your secrets, and mine I will tell to you, we will share our most intimate parts. I will give all that I have to you and only you. May our yearnings for each other never end or cease and may our desires fight away the beast.

The beast of jealousy the beast of lies, the beast of envy – the beast that I despise.

Tony Bethel

When we make love my touch will be soft and gentle, much like a dove gently landing on an olive branch. When I touch your golden brown skin – I know in my heart it won't be a sin, for when we saw each other I knew you would be my lover – that none could ever compare with your sweet beauty and love so fair. You are my love you are my heart. You are my beginning, you are my new start. When I touch you and you touch me I will be able to set the caged spirit free for my heart, soul, and spirit were bound – until you came around. Now my heart soars like a hawk.

When we make love…

You

Who is the girl that fills me with desire?

Who is the girl that sets my heart afire?

Who is the only one I would ever make love to?

It is you. It is you.

Who is the girl who would never leave my side?

Who is the girl that fills me with such pride?

Who is the only one whose love is true?

It is you. It is you.

Who is the girl that turned to woman?

Who is the woman that gave me a girl?

Who is the little girl that I now adore?

She came from you. From you.

Where is the woman I once held in my arms?

Where is the woman I once filled with my charms?

She has gone to heaven; but I will remain true.

For there will never be another like you. Like you.

I love you.

One Love

When I am away from you, I feel tired, sad and blue. Life has no meaning words have no place, in explaining your love, which is full of grace. You have become a part of me and me of you; I am certain your love is true. When I touch you I only want more, but I force myself not to explore. Being around you I lose my control, I fear for my heart, body and soul. The temptation is great, and yet your sweet kisses and soft touch soothes the burning, stinging, tearing, surging thoughts in my mind. I have such a great appetite, yet just being with you satisfies me. How can this be when all others had to give more? Investing in your love has made me grow from boy to man, from weak to strong, from wrong to right. Your love hits the spot. You refresh my hardened heart that was in doubt. You showed me that love can be, and your love has set me free. Without your love I was on the road to sin but receiving your love has breathed life into me again. Your love cures my wounds. When I am away from you I am a half looking for a whole — a body searching for a soul – a miner searching for gold. For I have been searching for one like you all my life and you are the first one I have found like you. My search is over now. So we must begin our life's journey with one another. More than a sister or a brother. More than a friend or lover. I don't have to seek another. We have become one flesh; one life; one goal; one love.

She Is A Woman Of Today

She is a woman of today.

She will never change her ways.

She knows what it was like before.

She wants to run her future and so much more!

She is a woman of today; Black, White, Hispanic, Asian, straight and gay.

She will let no one or nothing turn her away.

She keeps on the path with a sarcastic, cynical sort of laugh, determined to succeed- be it for love, ambition, need or greed.

She is a woman of today; and like her brother the male she no longer fears jail, to fight for what she thinks is right; or pursue love in the night.

She is a woman of today, intelligent, naive, innocent, seductive, strong, weak, feminine, sure, unsure, needing, demanding, thriving, hating, loving… woman.

Woman of today, never change your ways – I am in love with you just the way you are.

Tony Bethel

I Think About Your Love

I think about your love when the sun is about to rise; when I am half awake and the sleep is in my eyes.

I think about your love when I wash up in the sink.

I think of your sweet kisses of which I would like to drink.

I think about your love when I am shaving in the mirror.

I look for your reflection – but it does not get any nearer.

I think about your love when I am putting on my clothes. I think of your warm eyes and very cute nose.

I think about your love when I am walking out the door — a man as lucky as I could not ask for more.

I think about your love when I am standing in the chow line, and I am happy—oh so happy that you are always mine. I think about your love when I am sitting down to eat. I think of the tasty food and then I think of your treats – for when I am with you my heart is afire my hands burn with quickened desire, longing to touch your soft, brown flesh and knowing with you I am loved best. I think about your love when I dispose of my tray and of our love which will always stay –

stay through the tests of time.

I think about your love on the way to school; my fellow

classmates think I am a fool. But if they had the love I had they would

realize, that this type comes once in a lifetime. I think about your love

when I am in my class if my teacher catches me, my face he would

smash.

I think about your love on a ten minute break and enjoy every

minute… of what, I cannot say. I think about your love on the way to

class, and for all this sinful thinking I have gotta go to mass. When I

go home after school; what is on my mind? You! You! You!

From sun up to sundown, from every smile to every frown it is

You! You! You!

Now tell me if my love is not true. I think of your love when the

sun goes down; I curl my lips and then I frown. For I will spend

another restless night without your body by my side. I think of your

love when I go to bed and ending my frown, I smile instead thinking

of the sweet dreams in my head.

Tony Bethel

Open Your Mind to me:

Open your mind to me, let your words be as honey on bread.

Open your mind to me, let your hands rest upon my head.

Open your mind to me, so deep and profound.

Open your mind to me, always breaking new ground.

Open your mind to me, life starts anew.

Open your mind to me – I think I love you.

My Woman:

Let me tell you about my woman:

Her hair is kinky, and beautiful in its limitless fashions.

Her lips are thick, their sweet taste envied by many men.

Her wit stings like the sting of a bee.

Her humor is light, joyous, and carefree.

Her warmth and compassion are beyond compare.

Her eyes have seen many sorrows, yet her spirit is a bright

ray of sunlight which could shine through a multitude of dark clouds.

She is graceful and quick, much like a gazelle.

The way she carries herself, she is a lady as well.

Her skin has many colors but they all are Black.

Her mind has many facets and her love has many admirers.

All want to touch her, but her heart is no man's.

All want to rule her mind, but that—belongs to her.

All want to dampen her spirit, but her fire cannot be doused, her horse

cannot be tamed, and her determination cannot be stopped.

Tony Bethel

Free

Here I sit, worlds away, wanting you, day by day.

Separated by sight and sound, wanting your love, my heart steadily

pounds; Never realizing that which must be.

But for true love to blossom, it must be free!

Breaking chains of loneliness

Breaking chains of sadness.

Striving for happiness, save me from this madness.

Look into the looking glass and look at what you see –

A man bound in many chains, longing to be free.

Love is Blind

Why does your heart break time after time? Why are you crying

all the time? A new lover you need to find. But you say "No!."

"Love is Blind"

Why do you allow him to hurt you so? His emotions he never

shows. His affection for you is so slow. Why do you let him waste

your time… "Love is Blind"

Why on Earth do you suffer so, the abuses and uses of such a fool.

Do you realize that cruelty is not good for you? It reddens the eyes

and sags the cheeks it tears your heart making you feel weak. When

will you realize he is playing with your mind… "Love is Blind."

Your attraction to him I cannot understand He is the envy of many

a man. For your precious love, I would do anything Yet your eyes

won't see. I look into your bright brown eyes, and it always comes as such as a surprise; that eyes so knowing, loving, caring and kind,

could ever be so blind.

When love was just a notion

When love was just a notion, I thought much

of you, and of our entangled desires that

flow from me to you.

When love was just a notion, you sat upon my

knee and told me of emotions which could

set my cold heart free.

When love was just a notion, I thought of

other girls too; but time after time my thoughts

come back to you.

When love was just a notion, I wanted so much

to be free, but the thoughts of your sweet love

refuse to set me free.

When love was just a notion, I figured you

were the best thought in my mind, and the

thought of loving you would last

throughout all time.

Love Unheard Is Love Unsaid:

You look into my eyes of brown, I look into your eyes of blue, we have shared many a time—many good feelings between me and you. Yet all of this woe and dread, for love unheard is love unsaid.

I touch your hand, you touch my mouth. I turn my head and feign a cough. Afraid of the feelings within; knowing that I cannot win. Society is against us and these times are so unkind. A love like ours is not accepted yet it is very hard to find. Yet without you I would rather be dead, for love unheard is love unsaid.

I cannot accept what people say when I walk with you. I cannot accept the evil stares that cut you through and through. People tend to criticize and ostracize things they cannot understand, yet our love is the simplest— between woman and man. It is so annoying to live in such a place, which has so much room, yet will not allow you space. My heart is full of lead, for love unheard is love unsaid.

There are many like us, yet few come out, their love is doomed and destined to gloom. Yet those who stick together and fight against the tide, can hold their heads up high with dignity and pride. Why do so many believe the prejudice they are fed—never realizing; love unheard is love unsaid.

We spend a lifetime picking others apart, condemning their lives like men without hearts—never realizing we are all each others parts. A concept so hard to comprehend, yet simple enough to the common man. Why do we waste time in others trivialities when we have such a decaying society. So many people alone, yet there are so many people. So many people bound to ideas which chain them to the ground which makes their hearts like stone—why do they choose to be alone. Should it matter who I choose to wed…for love unheard is love unsaid.

Tony Bethel

She is not the woman she used to be:

She, is not the woman she used to be, her eyes are dull and her hair hangs free.

Once a radiant smile illuminated her face, but now a wicked frown has seemed to replace it.

Her once carefully trimmed nails have turned to claws.

When I look at her now – I find many flaws.

Her wardrobe was once filled with bright and lively colors; but now-black is the only color she knows.

I loved her for her beautiful and magnetic personality; now, I am only magnetized.

She draws me near, yet I am repulsed by what I am attracted to. I want to leave her, yet something strange and mysterious binds my heart to hers.

Her eyes once warm have grown so cold; they now are piercing-penetrating my soul. They are like icy lasers which freeze my mind and insides.

I want to break away, but I can only cry; for if I cannot free myself from her "love"… I will surely die.

Is there any escape? Any solution? I feel my soul's steady dilution. It is too late! I shall never be me…

Because?

I am not the man I used to be.

Tony Bethel

She's a Vamp

I feel the strangeness of her touch, something cool attracts me. I feel the strangeness of her love, somehow I don't feel free. Her face chiseled, a pale marble white, yet ruby red lips which kiss a sweet goodnight. Her eyes are like coals burning in fire, and when I see her I cannot avoid intense desire. Long flowing tresses of Raven Black hair, yet she wears a silky white gown – a great contrast there. I look into the mirror, but her, I cannot see, is it something we drank which so intoxicates me. She sits on the couch to get warm and cozy, I notice a flush in her cheeks, which are now red and rosy. She sighs, leers at me, telling me she has a surprise. She begs, even pleads, that I should close my eyes. Then she slowly tilts my neck to one side and releases wildly, a passion she can no longer hide. Our hearts beating frantic, filled with burning desire; as her teeth sink into my neck I should have known

– a vampire.

Defeat:

At the end of the tunnel Defeat waits for for me, with a never ending smile filled with happiness and glee.

At the end of my journey when my feet are worn and back is sore, Defeat waits on the corner with the smile of a whore. I can never buy you, because you will never be mine, but the whore says "You may still try, try, try..."

I try to escape and run away, yet defeat dogs me every step along the way. Defeat seems to know where I hide, and seeks to take my dignity and pride. Defeat, Defeat, please leave me alone, my bones are brittle and my heart is torn. Defeat just laughs and breaks my heart, leaving my spirit low, looking for a new start; seeking a new goal; trying to lift my weary soul from the battle torn fox hole.

Defeat, Defeat, why are you so unkind, why do you try to destroy my body and my mind—must you be so greedy, could you at least leave me with one? Defeat laughs and says, "That is the way of the world my son." Is this my fate and destiny, to have my hands bound—

never more to be free. Fate, Fate, why are you so unkind. You and Defeat keep me so far behind.

When I open my arms and reach for the stars, Defeat once again cuts off my arms, and breaks my dreams. What is a man to hope for, when life unravels at the seams?

How can I find my destiny, when Defeat will not let me be.

I could fight with the competition of Defeat, but it is the repetition of Defeat which kills my heart, with a slow poison as thick and resistant as oil. Defeat, Defeat, have mercy on me; let me live and be free. Defeat says "That is not possible", because Defeat is after a man's soul. Defeat pushes you to the brink, and hopes your heart sinks so low and so abysmal into the fiery depths, that the only resolution in one's mind is the "final solution" of one's self, of one's being and of one's essence. Defeat wants us to take our lives, because Defeat alone cannot take life, it can only cause pain and strife. It is you, who must want to die, for Defeat alone cannot kill.

So Defeat, you are unveiled, and left exposed. I fear you not, for my soul is a rose—and for each failure you fire at me, my soul blossoms endlessly. For with each new mistake, I learn a little more—

for each rejection, there is always another door.

Yes, Defeat waits for me at the end of the tunnel, but it is I who

wear the smile—not he. For faith in me, has set me free.

Honesty:

I was sitting here wondering why people lie. We cover up so many important things; then we curl up and die—leaving a legacy of lies. We hide behind a veil of steel, not letting others know us for ourselves. We deceitfully hide in metal shelves; cold, hard, pointed and sharp. We keep our heart under wraps, but when it comes time to give, we are out of sap — empty like a hollow tree, we hide again from honesty.

So many emotions, yet none are allowed to be seen, for we fear others will not understand what we mean. Running away again and again, never realizing honesty is a friend. Honesty keeps our hearts and minds open, never fearing to tell what must be told... cannot be bought with silver or gold; and under pressure, never folds. There are so many benefits to honesty, but to tell others is like telling a blind man how to see. We must want to be honest, to open our eyes, end our blindness and kill our lies. Only then will we see—what fools man can be. We play a game of hide and seek; we are found because we reek, smelling of a foul stench, which develops when lies commence. You

may run but cannot hide.

Oh fie! Oh fie! To be caught in a lie. You hang your head and sigh,

wondering why? You feel so small; so cold, you try in desperation to

dig a hole. Honesty looks you in the face and tells you why. Honesty is

not sly, or wry, *yet can make you cry... brings you to your knees...*

makes you beg and plead. To be exposed for a past crime you want to

lock honesty away and embrace the lie; but honesty will escape and

seek you out. Day by Day your haste to escape, you will throw lies in

its way. This will not stop honesty; for its desire for exposure, stays

calm, keeps its composure. Waiting as a Vulcano waits, the lava

builds, and so does the lies, when it spews, many will die. You ask

your friend the lie "what to do?" But you see, the lie cannot help you.

You lay lies down like dominoes, yet as the touch of the finger,

honesty will come and the lies will tumble, one upon the other until

there is a big jumble of overturned pieces. You mumble and mumble—

honesty will make a man humble.

Tony Bethel

When I Am Depressed

When I am depressed the world crashes all around me, my emotions so diverse they confuse, arouse, and confound me.

When I am depressed I sit alone, waiting for the tide to subside.

When I am depressed no one could possibly be on my side

When I am depressed I wonder what I was put here for.

When I am depressed I feel unwanted, unloved and ignored.

When I am depressed I wonder about this ugly world, with its ugly people doing their ugly chores.

We spend our lives day in and day out, with repetition so fierce, it would make a mute shout.

Yet, when I am depressed, I am more aware, of a better place – someplace out there.

The Silence Runs Deep

In these times when I am alone I think about the silence which runs deep within my soul. The silence which runs deep and rapid. Like an underground cavern which speeds unnoticed through the earth, the silence races through me when I am alone. I feel the in rush of thoughts, and questions about the universe. I sit in wonder and awe of the great mystery before me which had no beginning and hopefully no end. I feel the silence running through me like the unseen electricity flowing through the wires. The power is there yet inconspicuous to the eye. I feel the power of silence in me. Learn to feel the silence in you.

Tony Bethel

It Is No Fun To Grow Old

It is no fun to grow old, to feel the brittleness of the bones. To see the dry cracked lines in the face. To ache with every other pace.

It is no fun to grow old, to lose one's fight – no longer bold. Not appreciated for being around, having all hopes dashed to the ground.

It is no fun to grow old, the grim reaper knocks upon the door, he knocks repeatedly, more and more.

It is no fun to grow old the house and furniture are sold, time to go to the "old folks home", throughout the halls you see them roam. Once bright and active minds which somehow get pushed aside. Locked into a place in the past, the thoughts are painful and never pass.

It is no fun to be old… abandoned by everyone not able to recognize a son, no longer remembering the names, your destiny will be the same… for all Life's players, this, is the end of the game.

The Children of the Night:

They are the children of the night. They know how to drink, dance, and fight, They lurk under the murky lights waiting for prey, fearing the light of day. The ghetto sounds are in my mind, the talk of the street corners are so unkind. Men without jobs full of despair. Children wandering, yet, going nowhere. Schools which look like abandoned buildings. The vacant lots — home of the hoodlums. The projects look like prisons, yet the inhabitants are all American Citizens. Aliens in their homeland; outcasts and ignored, exasperated and bored. Life holds no surprises, holds no rewards—the punishment seems to have been born. Old Lady! Old Lady! Why do you cry? The pain and suffering shows in your eyes. You stand tall and proud like a stately queen, yet reality has crashed, and dashed your dreams. You go in and out of each day, clinging to your dignity. In you lies renewed hope of the days of Kennedy and King; of love and peace; of a world reborn—not carelessly ripped or unjustly torn. Your sadness shows, yet your hope grows. It is your light that fights these children of the night. To each little child you see, you say these words so convincingly:

"You can be what you want to be!"

"You can be what you want to be!"

If it is with love we fight, we can create the light, and the children of the night — will be no more.

The Revelation

I AM Big Brother, the Social Engineer, the one in your mind, the

one who people fear. YOU say I'll be here at the end of the world.

But I am ALREADY at YOUR front door.

KNOCKING!

KNOCKING!!

KNOCKING!!!

Oh let me in, you have NOTHING to fear. I will rearrange this

society; Program YOU perfectly; you will see.

I AM Big brother, listen to ME and I'll set you free

No MORE "WHITE is right!"

No MORE "BLACK is Beautiful!"

666 Just a NUMBER for a name; don't you like THIS game,

They call me Big Brother, I will provide for all! No rich No

poor... why don't you OPEN your door??

I am KNOCKING!!

KNOCKING!!!

I am Big Brother, you will never have to worry as for EVERYTHING you EVER do I will ALWAYS see!!

I am Big Brother, I EVEN have brothers today!! They are called the POLICE, the F.B.I. and C.I.A.

I AM Big Brother, let ME program your minds – let ME adjust YOU AND PUT YOUR "horizontal" back in line.

I AM Big Brother, so do as I say-OR my SECRET agents will come take you ALL AWAY!

I am Big Brother LISTEN to my heed—"This world will be destroyed due to RACISM, ARROGANCE, and GREED.

I AM Big Brother, but ME in CONTROL! I will take their minds AND TO HELL With their SOULS.

Give ME the Computer Chips and ENGINEERS galore! And I'll

turn this world around (for the BETTER)

F O R E V E R M O R E

!!!

I AM Big Brother, trust ONLY in ME, for only through me can

you truly be free.

I AM KNOCKING!

I AM KNOCKING!!

I AM KNOCKING!!!

I AM W A I T I N G W A I T I N G W A I T I N G

I AM HERE!

Tony Bethel

Black Is Beautiful! But...

Black Is Beautiful! But my legs are tired! I once marched, but I'm losing fire! I was once a fighter don't you see, but those Corporate Bastards got the best of me. You know, those white collared dudes who obey their laws, who make things sooo perfect, without any flaws; who simply exclude people like you and me. Those Corporate Bastards never learned to see!

Black Is Beautiful! But my arms are tired! I once held pickets and boycotted firms! But those Corporate Bastards look at me as if I have germs. We once fought valiant for our rights back then, But good ol' Conservatism wins again!

"The Liberals; they spend too much can't you see?!
There is not enough left for Rich men like me.
That is why I'm glad George is in there now –
He will show those people, Oh boy and how!!!"

Black Is Beautiful! But my back is tired! I have been bruised in so many "riots"! Remember those uprisings when things got bad, when economic equality could Not be had. We fought back Then and we'll fight again! But those Corporate Bastards will be ready by then! Ready with Guns; and Ready with the Chains;

Sounds just like—

"The Good Ol' Days"(?)

Standing All Alone:

Standing all alone on a street corner.

Standing with a gun in hand… do I really want to?

Standing with his back towards me, I wonder will he feel, the blazing hot lead, the shattering of steel.

Standing all alone now, once two — now are one.

Standing all alone now with the smoking gun, looking at the bloody corpse…

"One less in prison"

When The Last...

When the last slum is torn down — That is when I will end my frown!! That is when I will end this hate, which is keeping me at Hell's gate. That is when I will rejoice — with a loud voice...

That there is a God!!!! — When the Last slum is torn down.

When my brothers are not beaten any more, for being brothers.

When my sisters are not raped — I will end my frown.

I will stop looking down

When we are not locked out of neighborhoods and schools because it ain't so cool (no more) to have Black faces around — No more!!!!

So, I think I know the score.

I think I will keep my frown.

Unlucky 13:

Thoughts of Blackness, running through my my mind.

Thoughts of Blackness, some cruel, some kind.

Thoughts of Blackness, help me through the night.

Thoughts of Blackness, prepares me for the fight.

Thoughts of Blackness, thoughts of home.

Thoughts of Blackness, my heart dares not roam.

Thoughts of Blackness, here today.

Thoughts of Blackness, Tomorrow dares not wait.

Thoughts of Blackness, my woman, my dream.

Thoughts of Blackness, colors from ebony to cream.

Thoughts of Blackness, are no longer there.

Thoughts of Blackness, unlucky it seems. Thoughts of Blackness, unlucky 13.

Why Must It Be

Why must it be that children starve while farmers have plenty?

Why must it be that others have so much while others don't have any?

Why must it be that certain people of certain colors can't be free?

Why must it be that others are so blind while others can truly see?

Why must it be that bombs and arms have more importance than

food? Why must it be that some are non-violent, while others are

violent fools. Why must it be that men worship many Gods, yet, kill

each other violently in the name of God. Why must it be that women

are treated so cruel, they have come from man, yet man uses her as

tool?

Why must it be that man has more faith in a machine, than in his

fellow man, whom he chooses to treat so mean?

Why must it be that some men live in big houses on tree-lined

streets, while others wander, in the streets?

Why must it be that some men have clothes for several men, while

several men have no clothes. Lord, why must these things be? When

will man be free? When will we have enough to eat? When will you bring us home? When will we cease to roam? When will you send your son? When will our judgement come? Even though I have love and faith in thee—I still wonder…

Why must it be!?

My Heart Is Burning, Yet My Tongue Is Silent

How can we live in such a world filled with hate. How can we have this block to communicate; when the future of the world is on the line, our lives – both yours and mine. Even after all the violence, my heart is burning, yet my tongue is silent.

How can we live in such a world of deviates and psychopaths – I hear their morbid laugh. I hear a woman's scream and I know they have shattered her dreams – and where did her purity go?! She was violated in the building next door. How can we allow this to be, – "the land of the brave and home of the free." Even after the violence, our hearts still burn, yet our tongues are silent.

How can we live in such a world of lies, where truth is abused, hated, and despised. How can we teach our children well when they hear the lies we so often tell. So many lives lost in vain, so many faces – no one remembers the names. So many soldiers fighting for the truth; but the truth is lies – just ask the spies. So hard the war was fought; and for naught. So, when will enough be? That is up to you and me. We must all end the silence, and with all our hearts, burn the violence.

Time For A Change

In these times of trouble, in these times of doubt, I stand here wondering – will this world win out? With its violence and need to rearrange don't you think it is time for a change?

In this world of cynics, snobs, fools, me and you, don't you think we could just for once come together and see this through. Instead of "shooting now and taking names" have you asked yourself "What about time for a change?"

In these time of child abuse, wife abuse, and parent abuse …when will love get some use? When can we hope for a brighter day – instead of looking for higher pay. In this world what should we seek, when every thing good is made to reek. When all ideals are shot to the ground, nothing to look forward to, each day is the same. Don't you think it is time – time for a change?

Tony Bethel

Black Hands

Black hands which toil in the field.

Black hands which struggle refusing to yield.

Black hands working on machinery

Black hands loving me tenderly.

Black hands held high in protest.

Black hands that thrive for the quest.

Black hands which feel burning desire.

Black hands which have burned in many fires.

Black hands which have fought in wars.

Black hands chained from robbing stores.

Black hands tied and bound.

Black hands falling heavily to the ground.

Black hands bloodied from vicious dog bites.

Black hands floured from baking tonight.

Black hands carrying pickets striving for their rights.

Black hands on the terminal set.

Black hands remember, do not ever forget.

Black hands forever rising out of the mist all fingers together; forming

a fist!

Tony Bethel

I Am Sad To See The Little Children

I am sad to see the little children begging in the street.

I am sad to see the little children who have not had enough to eat.

I am sad to see the little children beaten and abused.

I am sad to see the little children sexually misused.

I am sad to see the little children with no shoes on their feet.

I am sad to see the little children whose parent's are deadbeats.

I am sad to see the little children without decent clothes.

I am sad to see the little children from broken homes.

I am sad to see the little children who fight in the street.

I am sad to see the little children being sold like meat.

I am sad to see the little children getting on drugs from family frustration, economic depression, and desperation.

I am sad to see the little children having little children, who will have little children…

I am sad to see the little children's parents living on aid, unable to find work in a world GOD made. How, oh how can this be – when we pray to the saviour to set us free.

I am sad to see the little children with their cold, cold eyes; which will grow up to hate, rape, kill, and despise.

I am sad to see the little children with beautiful brains being held back because their ambitions have no aim. When I die, will anyone remember my name? Will the cycle be broken – or will it stay the same?

I am sad to see the little children shoeshining for a nickel, maybe a dime and people wonder why they turn to crime.

I am sad to see the little children afraid to go to school; because they want to learn, and learning is not "cool".

I am sad to see the little children breakdancing on the corner. their bodies so limber, their limbs so agile, the pride in their movements… But God what about their minds! Their minds! Their minds!

They are mine! My people, my people, oh beautiful people, don't let your pretty flowers turn to weeds; hear my words and take my heed. Save the little children – for they are our treasure, our hope our future.

Tony Bethel

The Paradox

W-White   B-Black

W   Is it true what they say about those people at that table?

B.   Why must *we* assimilate, why can't *we* just be *us* I *don't*
     understand this fuss; what should it matter if I could sit with
     Whites or *Blacks*-and I choose the *latter*?

W.   Don't *you* understand, *we must* be *unified* you see, so the Beast,
     Racism, will soon cease to be.

B.   *When* will *you* people understand, we have *nothing* against *you*,
     it's just that *you* try to *kill* our *culture*—and *that* will *never* do.

W.   *What* is this you say? *You're free in every way*; we have *no* chains
     on you, nor are you bond, too.

B.   It's *more* than what you say, we're *not free in every way, the*
     economy binds our hands; the *government steals* our lands; and

110

you tell me all I have to do is *sit* next to *you*; *who* are *you* trying to *screw?!*

W. *Don't* blame *me* for *this system, it* was here before I was born. *I* would *like* to be *your friend* and end this *series of doom.*

B. *You* say you want to be *my friend?!* Help *change this system* which *never* ends, which feeds upon *your* people, too; let's *change this system, me* and *you.*

W. We *can change this system,* sure we can, for *each* and *every man*; but *all* I'm asking of you is could you be my friend too?

B. *That* is *not* a *simple* question to ask. I see it as an *awesome* task, for after *all* the things *your race* has done—you say. *"Let's be buddies!" "Let's have some fun!"*

W. *I* cannot claim *total* innocence for *my race; certain* things *my race* has done makes *me* want to *hide my face.* But please, listen to what I have to say, "Why must *your* people *segregate*—in *each* and *every way?*" I know *whites* have *their* faults, too. But *what* makes *BLACKS* so *special*? Won't you tell me? *Yes*, please do.

B. To explain the *injustices* to *our* race would take an *infinity*, much more time than you or I will ever see. For *you* to understand what I do, *you* must walk the miles in my shoes. And in reflection *you* could see, that I am you, and *you* are *me—so what difference* does it make at which table I partake, since *color is* relative. Can't you see that *Underneath, I* am you and *you are me?* To answer your question straight and true, 'those people at that table' are *no* different than you other than the *skins* in which they be. But what should it matter; cause underneath, *I* am *you* and you are me.

I am my Brother's Keeper.

For those starving in Somalia, this, is for you. For those in America who sent money to pay their heavenly dues—what is life?
What is truth?
The lies get deeper—yet, I am my brother's keeper.

For those in China, this, is for you. Communism and Capitalism both embrace you
You wonder where the ideals are—at the point of a gun.
I thought with Communism, the people were number one?
The lies get deeper—yet, I am my brother's keeper.

For those in Ireland, this, is for you. You hate the British—Yes, that is true. They are only there to protect, guide and save you from yourselves. They have no interest in dominating or restraining you— is this, not true?
The lies get deeper—yet, I am my brother's keeper.

Tony Bethel

For those in the Middle East, this, is for you. You want guns instead of food; and yet, each day there hatred is renewed. Will Islam show the truth? On your knees to pray; more suicide bombers will die today. Yet, their souls will be saved—at least that is what the Koran said.

The lies get deeper—yet, I am my brother's keeper.

For those of this world, this, is for you. How long can we last, if we choose to blast and kill, to gain our "skill?" To bomb and maim—where do we put the sick and lame? One day the lies will get too deep, then there will be no more brothers to keep.

For those who served their country.

My Brother

I was the one who was good in school.

You were the one who was really cool.

I was the one with the degrees.

You had the friends and the money.

I was older, but you were wiser.

I was uptight, but you let it ride.

We were different like night and day but we both respected each others way.

We looked up to each other, both different, yet brothers.

"And the rockets' red glare"

Before the planes hit I begun to stare and then it happened, and I saw the rockets red glare. Americans all burned in that fire, some were foreign but they all had the desire.

The desire to be free. The desire to make it in America for themselves and family.

The American dream brings them here to see, but after 9/11 we realize there *is* a cost to be free. Christian, Muslim and Jew died in that fire too. Americans all, like me and you.

Before you look with hatred at others and begin to stare, remember our anthem, our ideals,

"And the rockets' red glare…"

For the victims of 9/11

For our Nation that survived.

Land of the Free

Land of the free doesn't that include me

the Muslim man in a beard who was born here.

Land of the free doesn't that include me

the Single mother of three working two jobs to make ends meet.

Land of the free doesn't that include me

the poor white guy over there sitting on the unemployment chair.

Land of the free doesn't that include me

the black guy right here who the police unjustly fear.

Land of the free doesn't that include me

You want to make me go but I was born *here* not Mexico.

Land of the free doesn't that include me

the one that is not straight, yet perfect in every way.

Land of the free let it not be hypocrisy, let us live

up to our creed and ensure all live free.

Land of the free…

For the victims of 9/11.

For the victims of intolerance.

Before 40, After 9/11

Age 40 is the time we make major changes. After 9/11 America will never be the same. I turned 40 this year. I remember 9/11 as though it were still here. The country has changed and cannot go back; and now at 40 I look at my tracks.

Am I going where I want to go?

This country asks the same question about going to war. I look at myself and have some regrets. I know I am not the same as when I was younger. I am wiser.

This country too is wiser since Viet Nam. Do we want to make the same mistakes as the Russians did in Afghanistan.

My body creaks and aches with my age. This country too aches for leadership not influenced by wealth and personal power. I may not be swift but I have traveled this road before…in the Persian Gulf War. Our people may be slow to react, but they know the road we are on and where it is headed. I am now 40 heading into the autumn years; let us hope we are not headed towards nuclear winter after 9/11.

Tony Bethel

For the children of 9/11 victims.

For the children of Iraq would died due to sanctions imposed.

About the Author

Tony has been writing poetry since the age of ten. His first book was *Love is a Butterfly,* which was a collection of poems dealing with various types of love and relationships in peoples lives. Tony attended the University of Illinois and received a bachelor's degree in Psychology (1983). He served nine years in the U.S. Navy (1983 – 93), and was in the Persian Gulf War. Tony now works in an Institution that enriches the lives of the developmentally disabled. Tony is also a licensed Physical Therapist Assistant and licensed Massage Therapist with a practice in Lombard, Illinois. Tony has three children who are a great source of inspiration. Tony's reason for writing this book was to reflect on the past forty years of his life and to share his writing with other Americans after the 9/11 tragedy.

www.ingramcontent.com/pod-product-compliance
Lightning Source LLC
Chambersburg PA
CBHW051441280526
45785CB00003B/1385